LAW & ORDER

JUDGES AND LAWYERS

Zachary A. Kelly

The Rourke Corporation, Inc.
Vero Beach, Florida 32964

© 1999 The Rourke Corporation, Inc.

All rights reserved. No part of this book may be reproduced or utilized in any form or by any means, electronic or mechanical including photocopying, recording, or by any information storage and retrieval system without permission in writing from the publisher.

PHOTO CREDITS:
Danny Bachelor: cover, pages 4, 6, 14; Tony Gray: pages 9, 19, 32; © Bob Daemmrich/Stock Boston: pages 12, 22, 24, 36, 39, 42; East Coast Studios: pages 16, 17, 26, 34; © Dana Penland, Smithsonian Institution/Courtesy the Supreme Court of the United States: page 29

PRODUCED BY: East Coast Studios, Merritt Island, Florida

EDITORIAL SERVICES:
Penworthy Learning Systems

Library of Congress Cataloging-in-Publication Data

Kelly, Zachary A., 1970-
   Judges and lawyers / by Zachary A. Kelly.
     p. cm. — (Law and order)
   Summary: Explains the roles of lawyers and judges within the court system and defines terminology related to their functions.
   ISBN 0-86593-577-7
   1. Lawyers—United States—Juvenile literature. 2. Judges—United States—Juvenile literature. [1. Lawyers. 2. Judges.] I. Title. II. Series.
KF8795.Z9K45   1999
347.73'5—DC21   99-6026
                                                                                      CIP
                                                                                       AC

Printed in the USA

TABLE OF CONTENTS

Chapter One
THE RIGHT TO REPRESENTATION 5

Chapter Two
DEFENSE 11

Chapter Three
PROSECUTION 15

Chapter Four
WHAT A LAWYER DOES 21

Chapter Five
JUDGES 25

Chapter Six
SUING IN COURT 31

Chapter Seven
DECIDING A CASE 35

Chapter Eight
FILING AN APPEAL 41

GLOSSARY 45

FURTHER READING 47

INDEX 48

Most cases involving crimes end up in a court of law.

CHAPTER ONE

THE RIGHT TO REPRESENTATION

A person accused of a crime usually has to go to court. Most people, however, do not know what to do or how to protect themselves in court. Therefore, the sixth amendment gives everyone the right to a lawyer's help. This right is called the *right to representation* because we are allowed to have a lawyer represent our case in court. Although we are free to represent ourselves in court, we can also get help from a lawyer if we are unable to do a good job on our own. This right holds two important questions: When in a case do we have the right to a lawyer? Do *indigents* (poor people) have a right to a free lawyer?

A lawyer appears in court with a defendant.

The sixth amendment meant the right to a lawyer only at a court trial. Over the years people have shown reasons for changing this meaning. Today our right to representation includes nearly every step of a case. The accused has the right to a lawyer during a lineup, at the arraignment, and at many other times.

> *In all criminal prosecutions, the accused shall enjoy the right to a speedy and public trial, by an impartial jury of the State and district wherein the crime shall have been committed, which district shall have been previously ascertained by law, and to be informed of the nature and cause of the accusation; to be confronted with the witnesses against him; to have compulsory process for obtaining witnesses in his favor, and to have the Assistance of Counsel for his defense.*

The sixth amendment to the U.S. Constitution assures a speedy, public trial for all accused persons.

An accused person's attorney may be present at the police station just after the person's arrest. The accused may even have a lawyer present before being arrested if the police are questioning him or her about a crime.

Indigent people often cannot pay a lawyer. But they still have the right to representation. At first the sixth amendment said that the accused had a right to a **retained**, or paid, lawyer. Then in 1942 the Supreme Court decided that the poor could have a free lawyer in all federal court cases.

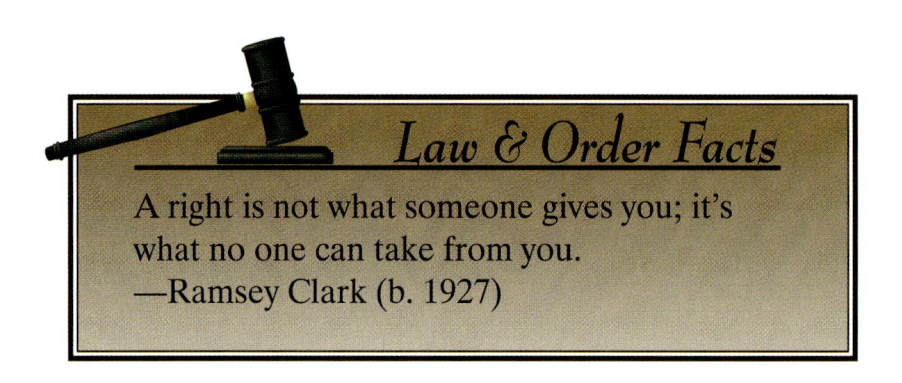

Law & Order Facts
A right is not what someone gives you; it's what no one can take from you.
—Ramsey Clark (b. 1927)

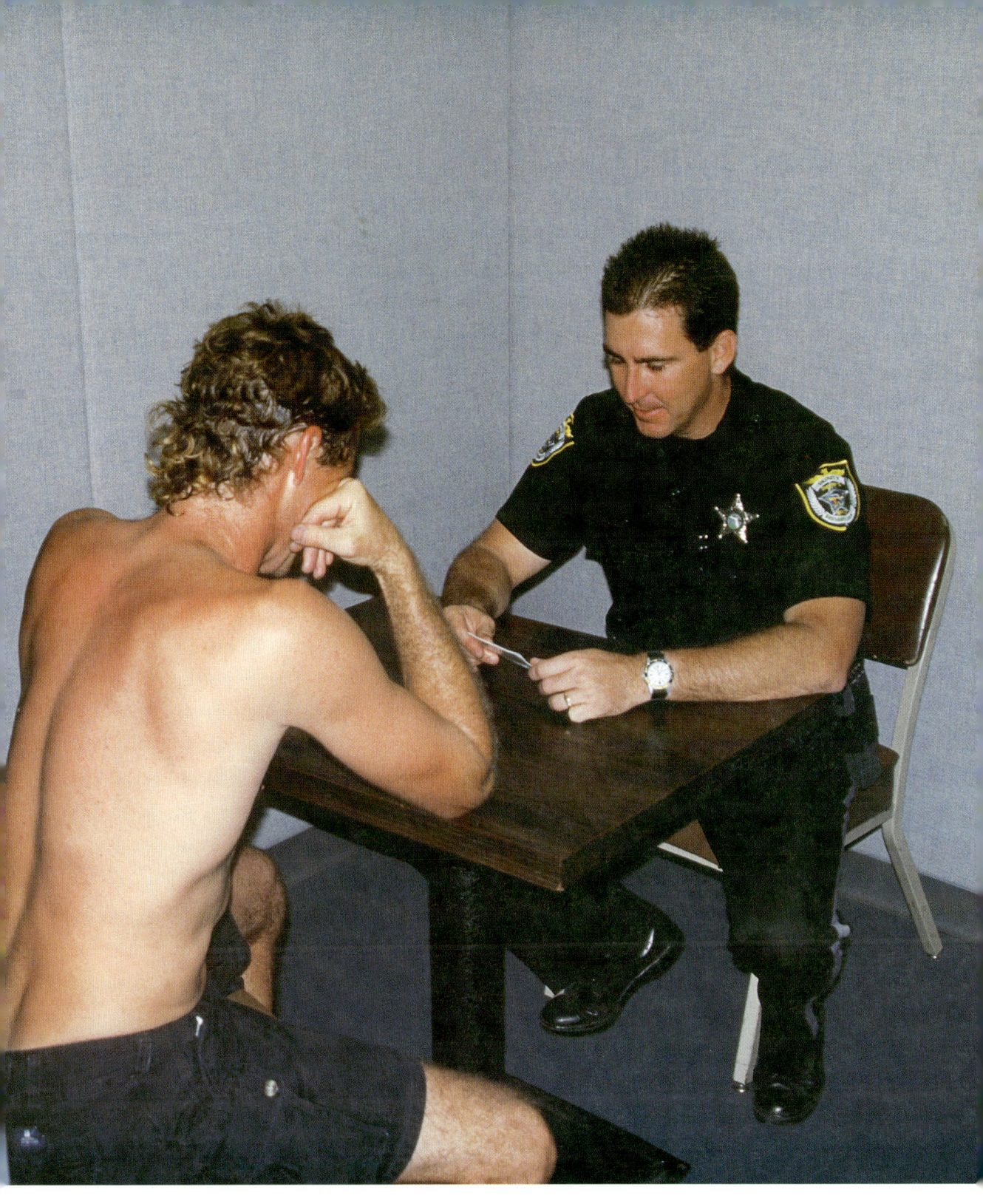

A police officer reads an accused offender his rights.

By 1972 most state courts also agreed that the poor could have a lawyer when accused. The courts can choose three different kinds of lawyers: public defenders, private lawyers, and retained lawyers. Public defenders are lawyers who work for a state office dedicated to defending the poor. Private lawyers are lawyers who represent poor persons for no fee. But they are not paid by the state. A retained lawyer is hired by the state with a duty to represent an accused person.

CHAPTER TWO

DEFENSE

Defense lawyers have important jobs, protecting the rights of accused people. Whether public defenders, private lawyers, or retained lawyers, defense lawyers must protect the accused in several ways. One way is by speaking up for the defendant. As a "friend at court," a defense lawyer looks out for the defendant's interests in court. Also, a defense attorney is an **agent** for the accused person. That means that the lawyer acts and speaks for the defendant. The defense attorney plans the steps to take in a case, as though he or she were the accused person.

A defense lawyer talks with an accused client.

A lawyer protects the accused another way: by acting as a **jurisconsult**. A jurisconsult is someone who knows a lot about law and shares it with the defendant. A jurisconsult tells a defendant what to say and do in court. A defense lawyer works hard to get an **acquittal** or a lesser sentence for a defendant. An acquittal is a not-guilty **verdict** from a jury or judge. A lesser sentence is an easier penalty when a defendant is proven guilty.

Defense lawyers may protect the accused by making no case at all for the defendant. This is a powerful defense, because it forces the prosecutor to make a

> **Law & Order Facts**
>
> The good lawyer is not the one who has an eye to every side and angle but the one who goes after your part so heartily, that you can get out of a scrape.
> —Ralph Waldo Emerson (1803-1882)

strong case against the defendant. By doing nothing but attack the prosecutor's case, a defense lawyer can show reasonable doubt in the prosecutor's statement. This way can work well because a guilty verdict can only come when the evidence of guilt is beyond reasonable doubt. Defense lawyers use many other defense strategies to help the accused, such as alibis (excuses), claims of self-defense or insanity, and claims of incapacity (like drunkenness). Any plan that raises doubt about the prosecutor's side of the case can work for the defendant—if it seems reasonable.

Defending is a very important part of our legal system, but very few lawyers choose to work as defenders. Only about 4 out of 100 lawyers in the U.S. act as defense lawyers. Why?

One reason is that criminal defense pays less than other areas of law. For example, public defenders earn about the same amount as police officers. Other kinds of lawyers earn much more. Private defense lawyers, too, earn less than most other kinds of lawyers. Many defendants (about 65 out of 100) cannot pay a lawyer. Many private defense lawyers take cases **pro bono** (for the good), which means they don't charge for the help they give. Defense work often means working with hardened criminals. Some lawyers just do not like to work with criminals.

Some individuals accused of crimes must be moved in leg chains to prevent escape.

CHAPTER THREE

Prosecution

Prosecutors are lawyers chosen to serve the state or federal government. While prosecutors do many tasks for the government, two jobs are most important. First, prosecutors carry out laws by studying the **charge** made against an accused person by police. The prosecutor then decides whether the accused should be tried for that charge or a different one, or whether all charges should be dropped. Second, a prosecutor brings the charge against a suspect in a criminal court. The prosecutor argues against the suspect before the judge and jury.

A prosecution attorney studies a case for trial.

When a suspect is arrested, the prosecutor must study the charge against that suspect. Before a suspect goes to court, the prosecutor decides how the case against him or her should go. The prosecutor has three ways to charge a suspect. The lawyer can go with the first charge—the reason the person was arrested. The prosecutor can drop the charge and send the suspect to a social program, such as a drug rehabilitation center, or he can drop the charge and let the suspect go.

This prosecution attorney presents his case against the accused in a court of law.

Law & Order Facts

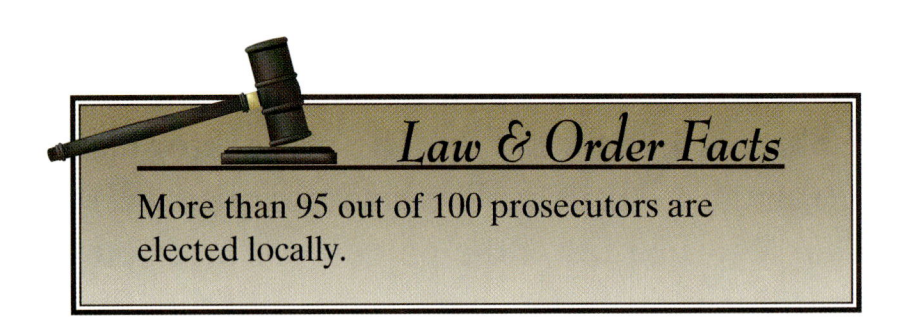

More than 95 out of 100 prosecutors are elected locally.

A prosecutor may write the police charge in different words, making the crime more or less serious.

A prosecutor knows how to uphold a suspect's rights while making a strong charge against him or her. A prosecutor works hard to show a judge and jury that a suspect is guilty as charged. To do so, a prosecutor uses all he or she knows about law and every legal means. Prosecutors and their helpers look for evidence and build cases against suspects. The prosecutor directs this work.

A lawyer becomes a prosecutor when citizens vote for him or her. Because prosecutors are elected, they represent the citizens who elect them. For example, say local people are greatly bothered by a certain crime. For the people, a prosecutor can make a very strong charge against someone accused of that crime.

A police officer puts evidence in a secure room. Later, the prosecution will use the evidence in a trial.

A chief prosecutor is in charge of a whole jurisdiction (area). Chief prosecutors usually serve four-year terms. Chief prosecutors in state jurisdictions are called **district attorneys**. Those in federal jurisdictions are called **U.S. attorneys**. Chief prosecutors have other prosecuting attorneys working under them. These attorneys are called assistant prosecutors. In some jurisdictions, they prosecute cases on a *zone* plan; in others, on a *case* plan. On a zone plan, an assistant prosecutor works in one courtroom, to which he or she is assigned by the chief prosecutor. On a case plan, an assistant prosecutor works all over a jurisdiction on assigned cases. Assistants prosecute cases according to two models, the zone model and the case model. In the zone model, an assistant prosecutor is assigned to a specific courtroom. The prosecutor is then responsible for prosecuting all cases that are tried in that courtroom. In the case model, the prosecutor is assigned individual cases from many different areas.

CHAPTER FOUR

WHAT A LAWYER DOES

Lawyers can do many jobs other than working as defense lawyers or prosecutors. One of the most important jobs lawyers do is to study and interpret (explain the meaning of) laws. In this way, lawyers help us use and understand our laws. Many lawyers focus on civil law. For example, an attorney may work mostly with divorce and child custody cases. Others may work on cases in which people disagree about owning property and paying debts. Still others may write *wills* (papers telling where a person wishes his or her things put after death). Then they carry out a person's will in court after he or she dies.

A judge discusses a sentence with a defendant and her lawyer.

Some kinds of law are very special: business law, tax law, international law, and social law.

A *business* lawyer meets for many hours with other lawyers and people who own and run businesses. At first they may disagree about how one business sells its products. Or maybe one business owner wants to buy another owner's business. They talk about many things that are hard to understand before they can agree.

A *tax* lawyer knows everything about U.S. tax laws. In court, a tax lawyer helps people keep their money instead of paying too much tax—when they sell a house, for example.

An *international* lawyer learns the laws of other countries. He or she explains how those laws affect people in the U.S. and how our laws may affect people in other countries.

A *social* lawyer works to defend a certain part of our society. Some lawyers like to defend our environment (land, water, trees, and so on) from people who would ruin it. Others defend people in cases about their civil rights (rights of all U.S. citizens as written in the Constitution). All lawyers study, learn, and explain the laws they work with.

Most lawyers have a reason for studying so hard: They want to solve real-life problems for people, using what they know about laws. A lawyer is a translator. He or she translates (changes) a person's words into the language used in court. A lawyer is a teacher. He or she teaches people about the laws that concern their cases. Also, lawyers find new ways to solve difficult legal problems. All kinds of civil and criminal problems can be settled in courts when lawyers bring their knowledge and skill to bear. Because lawyers want to solve problems that affect us every day, they often go into *politics* (work as government leaders). Some lawyers try to get elected or named to government jobs so they can do good in society.

Al Gore, like many U.S. government leaders, attended law school before going into politics.

CHAPTER FIVE

Judges

The main job of a judge is to head up federal and state courtrooms. Judges affect just about every part of a criminal case—from a suspect's arrest to a criminal's release from prison. One of the first jobs in a new case is to set bail. A judge looks at the charge against a suspect and the suspect's record. Then the judge decides how much the bail should be. Later, during a trial, a judge keeps order in the courtroom, while the prosecution and defense make their cases. The judge must then explain the key legal ideas to the jury. Hearing the judge explain helps a jury decide about the facts of the case.

A judge looks over his notes before handing down a verdict.

Judges must often make hard decisions. For example, a judge must decide whether to let a defendant plea-bargain (plead guilty to a lesser charge in return for having a more serious charge dropped). In some trials, a judge must give the verdict—"guilty" or "not guilty" or "guilty by reason of insanity." If a defendant is judged guilty, the judge must sentence him or her. And the sentence must fit the crime. Judges also develop the law and make laws easier for everyone to understand. As judges decide cases, they affect the way other judges and lawyers see and use laws. That way a judge adds something to the U.S. legal system.

Law & Order Facts

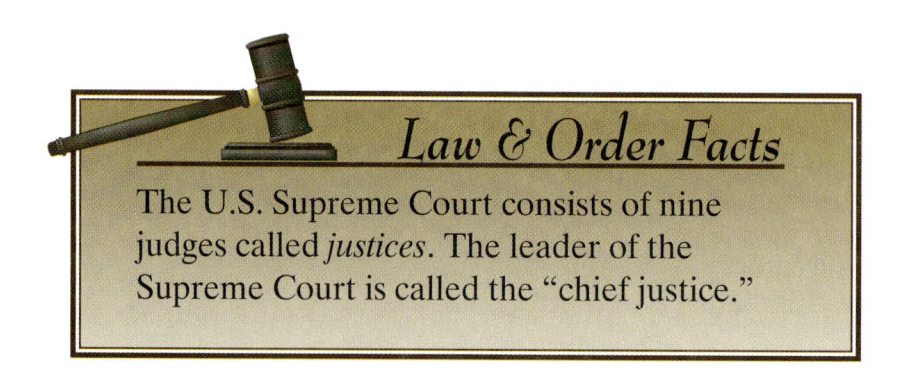

The U.S. Supreme Court consists of nine judges called *justices*. The leader of the Supreme Court is called the "chief justice."

Judges are chosen very carefully for their important jobs. A judge may be chosen in one of three ways. A judge may be voted in during a popular election. Thirty-three states use popular election to choose some judges. An election lets each citizen vote for his or her favorite candidate. But sometimes political parties can affect how people vote.

This sculpture of "Justice" is in the U.S. Capitol.

First woman appointed to the U.S. Supreme Court, Sandra Day O'Connor (1981).

A judge may be chosen by a group of political leaders who want him or her in that job. The person is appointed, or gets an *appointment*. Federal judges are appointed and so are many state judges. About 37 states now appoint some of their judges. Another way to choose judges is called the *Missouri plan*. The Missouri plan is an appointment—with some differences. It is even called a *modified* (changed) *appointment*. Under this plan, judges are appointed for one year. Then they are voted on during a popular election. The Missouri plan is good because it uses appointment and election. It gives political leaders and voters a say in picking a judge.

CHAPTER SIX

SUING IN COURT

The state prosecutes criminal offenders. If a civil law is broken the individual or group harmed sues the offender. Suing is the same as starting a lawsuit. Suing is also called *private litigation* because it involves private citizens rather than the state. A civil lawsuit is a violation of civil law brought to court. Two people or groups are always involved in a civil lawsuit: the plaintiff and the defendant.

Police officers assist the public with civil and criminal complaints.

The plaintiff is the person or group who believes they were wronged, and the defendant is the person or group accused of breaking a civil law.

The purpose of a civil lawsuit and a criminal trial are not the same. The purpose of a criminal trial: see if the defendant is guilty beyond a reasonable doubt of the charge against him or her. The purpose of a civil trial: see if the defendant owes the plaintiff for violating the plaintiff's rights. Plaintiffs usually sue for money. Courts often tell defendants they must pay the plaintiffs. Defendants may have to pay for damaging something the plaintiff owns. Or the defendant may have to pay the plaintiff's doctor bills or lawyer bills. In some cases the defendant pays to ease the plaintiff's pain and suffering. Sometimes defendants must repair the property damage they cause, instead of paying the plaintiff for it.

To start a civil lawsuit, a plaintiff or his or her lawyer files suit with the clerk of the court. Then the court sets a court date and tells the plaintiff to be there. Sometimes civil suits can be settled outside of court. A person called an **arbitrator** may help with an out-of-court settlement. Arbitrators can help the plaintiff and defendant agree without the expense and trouble of going to court. If this does not work, the plaintiff and defendant must be in court on the date set. A judge usually decides minor civil cases. A jury of six people is often called for serious cases.

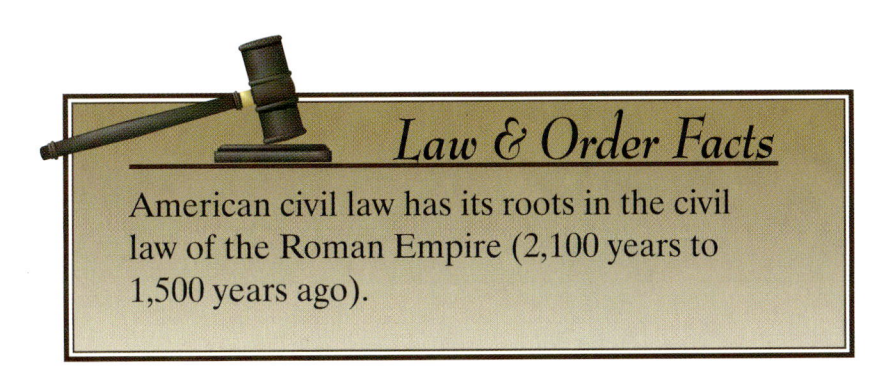

Law & Order Facts

American civil law has its roots in the civil law of the Roman Empire (2,100 years to 1,500 years ago).

To win a civil case, a plaintiff needs a "preponderance of evidence" to find the defendant guilty. The big word *preponderance* means the same as *outweighs*, or *weighs more*. To win a civil case, a plaintiff must make the judge or jury believe that the plaintiff's evidence outweighs the defendant's evidence.

If a case cannot be settled by an arbitrator, it must go to court.

CHAPTER SEVEN

Deciding a Case

Different kinds of cases are decided in different ways. Civil cases are decided according to civil law, while criminal cases are decided according to criminal law. In both kinds though, a judge or a jury gives the verdict. Usually, judges decide minor cases, and juries decide serious cases. In civil law, many minor cases are decided in *small claims* court. A small claims court takes cases about losses of a few thousand dollars or less. Small claims often have to do with buying and selling products and services. Most major cases are decided in a jury trial.

In a bench trial, the judge makes a ruling.

Minor criminal cases deal with *misdemeanors*, like *assault* (trying to use physical force) or *conspiracy* (an agreement to do an illegal act). More serious crimes—like murder and burglary (go in a building to steal something)—are called *felonies*. Anyone accused of a felony has the right to a jury trial. But an accused felon (person charged with a felony) can choose to have a bench trial, in which a judge, not a jury, decides the case.

Law & Order Facts

About a million lawyers and judges currently practice in the U.S.

Law & Order Facts

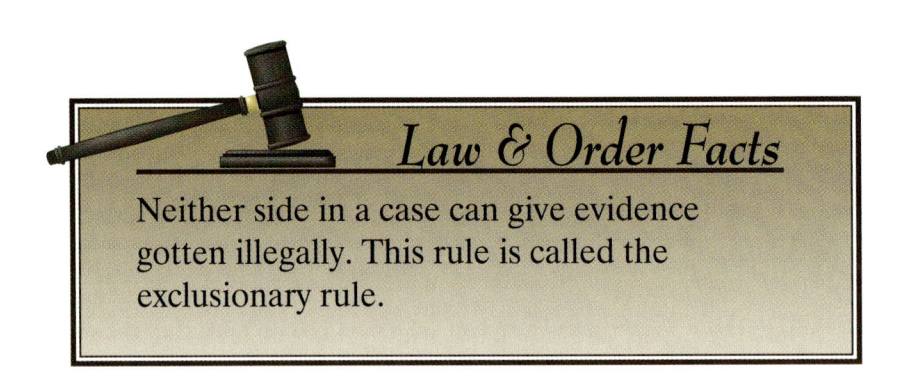

Neither side in a case can give evidence gotten illegally. This rule is called the exclusionary rule.

If a judge hears a case (civil or criminal), he or she takes certain steps to reach a decision. First, the judge listens to the evidence on both sides of the case. Second, he or she considers the evidence given by each side. Third, the judge studies the laws that are important to the case. Fourth, the judge decides and gives a verdict. Fifth, the judge sentences the accused if he or she is found guilty or releases the accused if he or she is found innocent. Following these steps, a judge can make fair decisions.

A civil or criminal case decided by a jury follows different steps. First, the jury hears both sides of the case. Then the judge charges, or tells, the jury about the laws in the case. The jury then leaves the courtroom. They go into a meeting room to talk over the case with one another. After discussing the case—which may take a few minutes, several hours, or many days—the jury votes. Most states require a *unanimous* vote (all jurors vote the same) to give a guilty verdict.

A jury listens as a lawyer presents her case.

If the vote is unanimous, the jury returns to the courtroom. One juror called the *foreperson*, gives the verdict to the court. Soon after, the jury decides on a sentence for the convicted (guilty) person. Sometimes juries do not get a unanimous vote, even after a long discussion. This situation is called a **hung jury**. In such cases, the judge calls the trial a **mistrial**. Then the judge sets up another trial with a new jury. After some mistrials, the prosecution may decide not to retry the case. Then the accused goes free.

CHAPTER EIGHT

FILING AN APPEAL

Proving someone guilty is called a *conviction*. The guilty person is a *convict*. A convict has the right to have a new trial if mistakes were made in the first trial. A new trial is called an **appeal**. The right to appeal protects convicts from mistakes the courts may make. Appealing is complicated with many steps. In the first trial, the defendant is innocent until proven guilty; but in an appeal, the burden of proof is on the defendant. Any court that takes an appeal is called an **appellate court**.

An attorney presents her case to an appellate court.

Appellate courts are the same as regular courts, but they hear appeals rather than first-time cases.

Every convict has the right to one appeal. He or she also has the right to a free lawyer at that appeal. These rights mean that all convicts can challenge a court decision. (To get more than one appeal, a convict must take certain steps. Only one appeal is his or her right.) The defendant must sign a paper listing all the mistakes made in the first trial. The first court then decides whether the mistakes are important enough to give an appeal. If the court agrees that serious mistakes

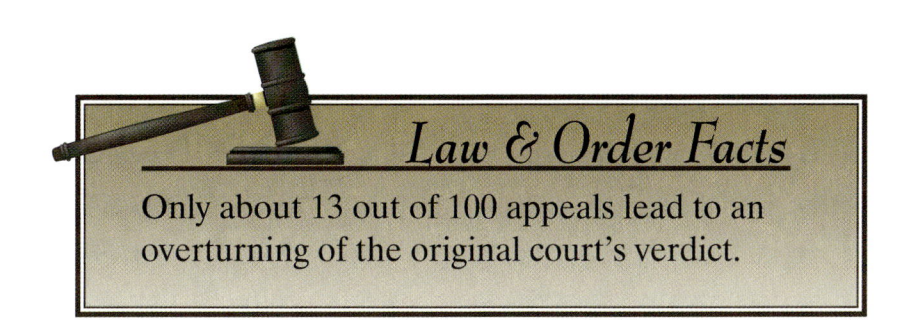

> **Law & Order Facts**
> Only about 13 out of 100 appeals lead to an overturning of the original court's verdict.

were made, the defendant gets a new trial. If not, the appeal is denied. The defendant must ask for an appeal within a certain amount of time after the first trial. If he or she asks later, no appeal is given.

Appealing a court decision involves several steps. First, a written request for a new trial must be sent to the court that convicted the person. That court can say yes or no. If the court says yes, the defendant's case is retried with a new jury. If the court says no to a new trial, nothing more happens. If the first court denies the appeal or if the second trial is faulty, the defendant can appeal to a higher court. The next higher court is the **state supreme court**. Appealing starts over at this level.

A defendant may stop appealing after the state supreme court decides the case. Some defendants appeal their cases to the highest court of all—the **U.S. Supreme Court**. This court takes appeals from all over the country that have not been settled in lower courts. Decisions of the U.S. Supreme Court are final—no more appeals.

GLOSSARY

acquittal (uh KWIT l) — verdict of a jury or judge that a defendant is not guilty

agent (A jent) — person with power to act for or represent another person

appeal (uh PEEL) — request for a new hearing

appellate court (uh PEL it KAWRT) — court system that takes appeals

arbitrator (AR bi TRAY tur) — person chosen to settle the disagreement between the plaintiff and defendant in a civil case before it goes to court

charge (CHARJ) — to claim wrongdoing against a person; to accuse or blame

district attorney (DIS trikt uh TUR nee) — highest prosecuting officer of a court district

hung jury (HUNG JOOR ee) — jury that doesn't agree on a verdict

jurisconsult (JOOR iss KAHN SULT) — person who knows a lot about laws; usually a lawyer

mistrial (miss TRIE ul) — trial that does not count because of a hung jury or mistakes in the procedure

GLOSSARY

pro bono (PRO BO no) — do without pay for the public good

retained attorney (ri TAYND uh TUR nee) — attorney paid for his or her services

state supreme court (STAYT soo PREEM KAWRT) — highest court in each state

U.S. Supreme Court (YOO ESS soo PREEM KAWRT) — highest court in the United States

U.S. attorneys (YOO ESS uh TUR nees) — the highest prosecuting officers of federal judicial districts

verdict (VER dikt) — the finding of a judge or jury in a trial

FURTHER READING

- Brown, Lawrence. *The Supreme Court.* Washington, D.C.: Congressional Quarterly, 1981.
- Conklin, John E. *Criminology.* Allyn and Bacon: Needham Heights, Mass, 1995.
- De Sola, Ralph. *Crime Dictionary.* NY: Facts on File, 1988.
- Hill, Gerald and Hill, Kathleen. *Real Life Dictionary of the Law.* Los Angeles: General Publishing Group, 1995.
- Janosik, Robert ., ed. *Encyclopedia of the American Judicial System.* NY: Charles Scribner and Sons, 1987.
- Johnson, Loch K. *America's Secret Power (CIA).* Oxford: OUP, 1989.
- Kadish, Sanford H., ed. *Encyclopedia of Crime and Justice.* NY: The Free Press, 1983.
- McShane, M. and Williams, F., eds. *Encyclopedia of American Prisons.* NY: Garland, 1996.
- Morris, N. and Rothman, D., eds. *The Oxford History of the Prison.* Oxford: OUP, 1995.
- Regoli, Robert and Hewitt, John. *Criminal Justice.* Prentice-Hall: Englewood Cliffs, NJ, 1996.
- Renstrum, Peter G. *The American Law Dictionary.* Santa Barbara, CA: ABC-CLIO, 1991.
- Territo, Leonard, et al. *Crime & Justice in America.* West: St. Paul, MN, 1995.
- *The Constitution of the United States.* Available in many editions.
- *The Declaration of Independence.* Available in many editions.
- Voigt, Linda, et al. *Criminology and Justice.* McGraw-Hill: New York, 1994.

- http://entp.hud.gov/comcrime.html
  Crime Prevention
  Department of Justice
  PAVNET (Partnership Against Violence Network)
  Justice Information Center
- http://www.fightcrime.com/lcrime.htm
  Safety and Security Connection
  The Ultimate Guide to Safety and Security
  Resources on the Internet
- http://www.internets.com/spolice.htm
  Police Databases
- http://www.psrc.com/lkfederal.html
  Links to most Federal Agencies
- http://www.dare-america.com/
  Official Website of D.A.R.E.

INDEX

acquittal 12
appeal 41, 42
appellate court 41
arbitrator 33
arraignment 7
business lawyer 23
charge 15
crime 5, 8
defendant 11, 12, 13, 14, 31, 32, 33, 34, 41
defense attorney 11, 12, 13, 14, 21
district attorney 20
international lawyer 23
judge 12, 15, 18, 25, 27, 28, 30, 34, 35, 38
juris consult 12
jury 12, 15, 18, 33, 34, 35, 38, 40
lawsuit 31, 33
Missouri Plan, The 30

plaintiff 31, 32, 33, 34
private litigation 31
pro bono 14
prosecutor 12, 13, 15, 17, 18, 20, 21
public defender 10, 14
representation 5, 7, 8
social lawyer 23
Supreme Court 8, 44
tax lawyer 23
U.S. attorney 20